THE CRASH WAKE AND OTHER POEMS

Owen Lowery was born in 1968. A British Judo Champion while still at school, he toured the UK and Europe competing and demonstrating. Before he could go to University he suffered a spinal injury while showing his skill for charity. He has since been tetraplegic. He gained a BA from the Open University, an MA in Military History from the University of Chester, and an MA in Creative Writing from the University of Bolton. He completed a PhD for Bolton joining creative and scholarly work relating to his own experience of living under perpetual threat of death to the World War II poet Keith Douglas. His Examiner for the Doctorate was Keith Douglas's Editor and Biographer Desmond Graham. His poetry has appeared in *Stand* and *PN Review*. He was listed for the Bridport Prize, the Welsh Open Poetry Competition, the Virginia Warbey Prize, and the International Sonnet Competition. His first Carcanet/Northern House book was *Otherwise Unchanged*. The artist Paula Rego, contacted through Anthony Rudolf, judged his poems relating to her work outstanding and she allowed her paintings to be part of his Carcanet book *Rego Retold*. He has read at the London South Bank, at many venues round the UK, and the BBC produced a TV programme about him. He married Jayne Winstanley whose love has been integral to much of his work. He recovered sufficiently from a car crash, that they both suffered, for him to produce the poems in this book. He had a sudden illness and died in May 2021. He was at that time preparing this book for publication, and many of his personal, present tense comments have been left as he wrote them.

The Crash Wake

AND OTHER POEMS

OWEN LOWERY

NORTHERN HOUSE

Northern House is an imprint of Carcanet

First published in Great Britain in 2021 by
Carcanet/Northern House
Alliance House, 30 Cross Street
Manchester, M2 7AQ
www.carcanet.co.uk

A CIP catalogue record for this book is
available from the British Library.

ISBN 978 1 80017 176 3

Book design by Andrew Latimer
Printed in Great Britain by SRP Ltd, Exeter, Devon

The publisher acknowledges financial
assistance from Arts Council England.

CONTENTS

Acknowledgements I   7
Introduction   11

The Crash Wake   15
Shielding   67
Someplace   68
Foxes   69
Seventh Anniversary   70
Owl in Lockdown   71
Past the Treeline   72
Before You Fly Home – Goa   73
From Post-op to the Ward   75
Kingfisher   76
Kicking in   77
Eid al-Fitr at the Martha Lutheran Church   78
Far Shore   79
Maiden Flight   80
Shoreline Sapphic   81
Shoreside   83
A Blackbird among the Berries   84
Poems from Transitions   86
Pictured – You Holding your Dad's Hand   93
You're Here   95
Love Island   96
Tribute   97
International Holocaust Remembrance Day   98
Ruth Dorfmann by Samuel Willenberg   100
Remembrance Day Sequence   101
Letter from a Private, Dunkirk   106
The Shark-singer   107
Backwash Parade   108
Aberfan Fifty Years on   110

Mermaid Drowning Wendy   111
The Blue Fairy Whispers to Pinocchio   113
Abortion Triptych, Left-hand Panel   115
A Birthday Poem for Paula Rego   116
Family Group at the Next Table   118
The Dance of Hunter and Prey   120
R.S. Thomas at Aberdaron   122
Stubbing Wharf at Hebden Bridge   124
Gymnastics – Rio 2016   128
Ode to You and Not Howard Webb   129
Snooker Commentary   130
Weak Light – Durham   131
A Sunday Morning in Cookham   132
F.D.R. Walks   134
Morecambe and Wise Show   135
Gardening Blind   137
Winter Rainbow   138
CC Footage of KW   140
Primark Socks   142
The Boats   144
Scotland as We Left It   145
Black Grouse   146
With the Fisherwoman of Nairn   147
Magpie Girl   149

Acknowledgements II   155

ACKNOWLEDGEMENTS I

This collection of poems has been created with generous support from Unlimited, Shape Arts, the Royal Literary Fund and the Society of Authors. I would also like to take this opportunity to thank my wife, Jayne, for helping me through such difficult times and for her unwavering love, patience and energy. Thank you also to my friends Michael Schmidt Anthony Rudolf, Jon Glover and Richard Berengarten, for their invaluable editorial advice.

To Jayne and Madison

i.m. Harold Earnshaw, David Lowery and Elaine Glover.

INTRODUCTION

These poems and this collection emerged as a result of a car crash, in which I was involved in February 2020. My wife, Jayne, and I were travelling to Scotland, for a week away, when our vehicle aquaplaned, spun round on the motorway, hit a barrier, flipped over the barrier and rolled over several times, before coming to rest on its side in a field. We then had to be cut free from the wreckage, a particularly complicated procedure, with my being in a wheelchair and dependent on a ventilator to breathe.

The car crash was very nearly fatal for us. I was left with three brain bleeds, a pulmonary bleed, and my right humerus was broken in three places. The process of recovery has been arduous, due to the cerebral impact. At one point I was having ten seizures a day and could not understand whether I was alive or dead. As I grew stronger and returned to creative work, it seemed only natural to try to make sense of the situation in which I found myself, through poetry. To add to the confusion, shortly after the accident, the coronavirus pandemic began to have an increasingly significant impact on life in general. Consequently, the crash and the pandemic became increasingly entwined in my emerging poems.

As must often be the case with any creative activity that takes place in a context of extremis, writing these poems has been challenging, not least because I tackled aspects of the car crash, and its psychological and physical repercussions. It has also been a cathartic experience, however, and has played a significant part in my recovery. The fact that myself and Jayne were both nearly killed, has placed greater significance on our relationship. Love, therefore, is one of the themes of the collection, set against the unfamiliar backdrop of the ongoing epidemic and the restrictions that were put into place as a result.

Since the surreal context exacerbated some of my mental symptoms, including dissociation and displacement, it made sense to adopt a largely extrospective approach to the poems, building on events as they unfolded, as part of my attempt to negotiate a way back to physical and mental wellbeing. Being disabled, ventilator-dependent and on the UK Government's 'high risk' register, increased my sense of social isolation, as well as raising questions about the situation of people with disabilities, with respect to medical treatment during the pandemic. For example, at the height of the crisis, the BMA released a statement in which they advocated a 'utilitarian' rather than a 'person-centred' approach to care, in which intensive treatment would be reserved for those deemed most likely to survive. My contacts within the health service have suggested that such decisions were based upon a 'frailty score', which has been alarming for many people. Therefore, these poems also examine the extent to which human rights have been and are being eroded, during the pandemic, and the way in which language is being used by authorities and media, in an attempt to create the impression that we are at war, rather than dealing with an epidemic.

In terms of format, this collection begins with a series of 104 twelve-line poems, followed by longer poems to end the collection. Mine and Jayne's combined age at the time of our crash was 104. The purpose of the shorter format for the opening series of poems was partly practical, as when I first returned to writing I had very little energy and had even forgotten how to use a computer. The shorter format also fitted the idea of taking extrospective 'snapshots' of the new environment in which I found myself, with themes rippling through the series of poems. The longer poems, on the other hand, have allowed for perhaps more in-depth considerations of recent events, hopefully, therefore, working alongside the shorter poems.

Because of the circumstances in which this collection was written, this is probably my most personal and, I hope, my most honest set of poems to date.

THE CRASH WAKE

1

Begin with us as we're helped, untangled
from ourselves, the field and sheen,
pure cold, until the strangeness
is our new world. Meaning

is you through whatever else, your voice
asking, first of all
like a child scared at having destroyed
its world, then urgent, calling

both in fear and hope. It will take time
and more to find our way
back to who we were before the shimmer
and promise of our snapped day.

2

The biting down is key, the locking
onto something more than air
and chemical sweetness. There for the looking
your messages and the first birds

through the window, speak, are spoken
for, as I fight a way
from vague to here. Waking, woken,
happen on the same delay

as yesterday. Wrapped in love I find
your promise among emails,
to come over later, defining,
being most of all.

3

Dealan-dè unpeels as I lie
between sensations, a flickering
dab of language taking flight
as read, unrestricted

and in every note of your voice as it breaks
the day. Knowing your hand
on mine as an instinct, one of the tracks
down which dreams expand

given time, strengthens and steadies,
works its own sweet
miracle. Again I want and need this,
love our absolute completion.

4

The need to go with it, hand in hand,
creates a whole new
world as I see us part of landscapes,
laughing a way through

impossibly brilliant green and blue
hills and shores. And I know
the confusion will be booming in soon,
sweeping off the glow

of a better year. But it's still us
I see, in whatever form,
separate and dancing to our own music
as re-imagined terms.

5

Call it a ghost from an ancestral side
as yet unexplored
but there's also something in the aesthetic, riding
a host of turmoils, the carrying,

almost taken like the latest
news, as if Westminster wants us
to care. For me, the strange teetering
between madness and sense continues

and spring yawns over roofs
and aerials looking west
from the bedroom window. Soon, I'll move in
and we'll hunt our lost pieces.

6

Spring to all intents and purposes
has clear skies and blossom
and the loose circling of a gull as it works
the air. Yesterday was for us

and to feel the sense returning to my words,
things clicking back
into place, watching whatever we were,
hand in hand, hatched

the hope that we might make at least a little
of what's ahead. Soon
perhaps I'll feel outside brittle
again on my reborn skin.

7

The glitter of blossom as it has been year
on year, folk-song-regular,
sparkles clear of your message. The garden
belongs to your mother, reaches

back, pops and fizzes. The birds
still come hoping
down, clattering over borders
as your words and meaning open

like summers. Between us we will get there
regardless. The mending happens
molecules at a time, an invisible stirring,
petals as crisp as paper.

8

We watch together another world
anchored around that contact
between our two hands, holding on
as we have before, only

now with each pleasure more
intense somehow. Having climbed
free and become this replenishing, tomorrow
nothing is what it seems

or will be from now on in. Complacencies
can rattle about in the mud
and wreckage as we make the future blaze,
emerge dazzled and renewed.

9

The grogginess slips aside, grudges me
more than a foggy view
until finally the words edge
clear. It's always you though

on the other side, as both idea
and destination, gleaming moment
and promise of more to come. To see
and feel you there becomes

everything. No doubt we'll laugh
again soon at the madness
of it all, the police cars warning us off
life on the main roads.

10

A grinning moon shares the night
with Venus, closer and clearer
than I've seen in a good while. Invited in
the night merges with our world,

with who we are and have been again
this evening. Your words
reconfirm, underline
your commitment to spare me the murdering

wards. I can breathe a little easier
perhaps, despite what we've seen
and heard coming through in pieces,
leave the night to serenities.

11

Gone today are the glass skies
we had yesterday, in favour
of a ruffling wind, a man twisting
an aerial on a roof and a gathering

of wood pigeons, with a fondness it seems
for the branches of the neighbouring mespil
tree. Soon I must attempt
a reply to a friend, in the most desperate

of circumstances. He wrote this morning to tell me
his mother had been put down
in a hospital in Granollers. What the hell
can you say? How do we respond?

12

It was her mother who it seems prepared the way
for her, cooking in a shimmering
version of the family kitchen. You could say
it was or wasn't as simple

as that, but for her there was no doubt
it was all as real as the rush
of those final injections. My grandad shouted
with joy before his great hush

came, saw someone or something
invisible to us. Coincidence
possibly, or the brain's response to the clumsiness
of death, but better than just blinking out.

13

I'm in the middle of writing back
when your message comes,
the timing as impeccable as ever. That knack
you have of knowing somehow

when most the love is needed flows
through, fills each letter's
flex and curve. On a day as salt-raw
as this, as immediate, you meet me

halfway, sweeten the loss. It will,
has to, get better
than this, doesn't it? You make me feel
and believe it will, at least.

14

A tree, depleted and leafless, and a lithe
flower where the shadow meets
the sun not only survive
my friend's message, but sweeten

the loss. It's all about revival
for him, the hope of life
beyond the now, arriving
so soon after his mother

had been put to sleep. We all need
something, I suppose. For me
it's always you helping to steady
and console, inspire and appease.

15

September prints itself on my mind
as a second chance at Scotland
after February's crash. The tender
turning of the first hot

leaves and those long golden evenings
promise more than we've had
in a while. Also, by then, we'd be forgiven
for thinking that the virus will be dead

or dying. Pure skies and a fortnight
of us untroubled and out of reach
to the world, living like we're nothing short
of immortals. That works for me.

16

Yesterday hangs heavy on me
this morning, difficult to shake off
against the vague backdrop. There'll be
more today, recoveries

and deaths, numbers for the newsfeeds to shout
high and loud. I'll take
the day as it comes, picture my shattered
arm coming back

to shape, wait on you writing
or calling in, watch as the world
drifts by, pretending it's alright,
and the latest butterflies uncurl.

17

A pair of swifts, presumably feasting
having travelled so far,
dart between moments, release
summer in their way. Comparisons

make themselves, tease the chances
of sharper and cleaner months
to come. That too of us answering
the need to return to something

akin to real life. Of course,
the butterflies will make a meal
as they blossom, snapped shut like stars
in a weight of universal velvet.

18

Any time, the geese should be clattering
over, finding their way
to the meres and marinas, revisiting those patterns
woven in the parade

of years. I always think of the joy
they bring with them, the buzz
you seem to get hearing their noise
at the petrol pumps, their rush

from an open window. Not quite music
I suppose, but pretty close
and something else that the latest news
is likely to miss out on or lose.

19

Fresh in, from the BMA,
official confirmation of how
they can intervene, choose which of us to save
and let go, weigh us all, like snowfall,

in terms of frailty, should any of us
be sufficiently unfortunate
to lie among the drowning rows
on the wards. Which of us is worth

what though? This I knew and feared
was coming. The rows of snuffed
lives stretch past my dreams, stare
through the darkness, unwavering.

20

Spring flows towards our autumn
adventure north of the border
as naturally as the throttle and gurgle of water
into the next container, disorder

into some sort of sense. Gold and red
come through, clearer
skies, a chance for us to need
and be needed in return. We'll repair

each other, grow beneath the gaze
of gentle hills, lie
together as if the world is so much gorse
or a trick of brittle light.

21

The weekend again lacks the rhythm
of matches and crowds. Virtual
horses ghost between courses, hover
in the nowhere region of dirtless

tracks. When the football does return
in all likelihood it will happen
behind closed doors. Morning
means birds and their hopeful

unlimited skies. Yesterday was us
spending time just being
together. Soon enough music
will build on that beautiful release.

22

It could be that there are fewer people about
but whatever the cause, there does seem
to be more movement among the sheltering
trees, more to scream

life in the face of eugenics. With evening
approaching, the skirmishing flights
continue, the late chorus delivers us
from a slightly shorter night,

brings outside in. Perhaps
even as far as our dreams
if we're lucky. There's a wood pigeon keeps
returning to the mespil's thicker stems.

23

They're burning masts up the road,
linking them to the virus. Seriously.
Not that I'm a great fan of the bloody things
either, but where do we score

the line? I've read the theories, been
largely ignored on the wards,
but do I believe in 5G
sparking the killer words?

Or imagine rather than believe. But I've seen
bony feet perched
on pylons and wires and heard the scream
of weather where cranes converge.

24

In Liverpool, the Beatles statues are masked up
along with others no doubt,
as the contagion drags on. The picture lasts
into my dreams, having caught me out

late on. You always find a way
to lift the mood, writing
shortly afterwards too to say
there's more to us than the tightening

screw of heavy news. I write back
in kind, love for love,
imagine where we touch. What we lack
we make up for and recover.

25

Nothing on the holiday cottage website
says pandemic. The hills
of Eildon roll past, throbbing
green after the silvers

and browns of winter. Patches of woodland
add darker and cooler
notes as we watch, look ahead
to September, imagine falling

from sleep into all that calm. We need
and deserve the peace, the chance
to rest, forget, relish the freedom
expressed in unquestioning glances.

26

The signs have been stripped from an Italian village
to keep the world away.
Soldiers man the boundaries like still
trees in winter, stay

where they're told with their lorries and masks,
both nervous and at ease,
each one a question mark
or a guess. Food has to be

brought in. Nobody risks the cordon
as the village searches for a rhythm,
tries to rediscover its ordinary
between life and death.

27

Another beautiful morning for heading out
teases projections of a summer
when we can once again bleed
into one another, assume

no harm in breathing, kissing, holding
hands. It is all glimmer
and dazzle, from the starry blossom, unfolding
a little more each time

I look, to the masts and aerials
on neighbouring roofs, the gloss
of pigeon throats. Simply to share
hours now is a blessing.

28

A Chinook flew past yesterday.
Today it was a Globemaster
C-17. Easter
looms at the weekend, untroubled

spaces, open roads, virtual
sermons and communions delivered
to photos on the pews of gaping churches.
There were army lorries by the quivering

lights of the local carparks too,
stranded like ice age
boulders at the fringe of time with you,
or like cast-off shopping bags.

29

Everything from the hawthorn to the scented
azalia seems poised
for the outbreak of summer. The greater intensity
in every shade, in the bird-noise,

after so long pupating in bed,
leaves me needing and wanting
more. Cuttings and borders shed
their dark, set about flaunting

restrictions of their own. We hold on, hold
out for better from the seasons
to come. Each loaded bud
strains to answer the summons.

30

Deer investigate empty streets
and not just at Chernobyl
now, edging in from the margins, meeting
their reflections in the windows. The sob

of birdsong not only wakes me
but invades the dusk. A quick
breeze dances through the breaking
buds. The talk of peaks

goes on amidst the morbid interest
in the latest deaths. It will end though
perhaps this side of next winter
painting fresh landscapes for us.

31

They're digging trenches in New York
to catch the tumbled bodies
at the same time as they try to talk us
into flattened curves. The loaded

language is pre-prepared. The gestures
too. Statements are delivered
in front of flags, as much guesswork
as anything else. Belief

binds onto hope. They can't hear
a thing up there for the buzz
on the nervous lips. We're not at war
but you'd never know by the voices.

32

Easter Sunday begins with a flashback
to that moment when our world
froze, the slowed time of the crash,
the crack of metal being pulled

and clipped apart, the taste of cool
fresh air and your voice
hardly daring to ask. You'll call in
soon, as sweet as music

and coming round to find you by my side,
guiding me back home.
Tell myself we're safe and it recedes,
crumbles back to dream.

33

And like that the best of the blossom has gone
the way of lost years,
lifted perhaps by the westerlies blown
off the Irish Sea. Spare

bark trembles and springs back,
catching the changes as they come
gusting in. Bit by bit my fractures
must be closing in their gloom

but how are we supposed to know
whether the bones will ever
re-align? You'll be glowing
when you get here, breeze on your breath.

34

And in another universe
Laurie Lee returns
to Slad. It is as it always was.
The ghosts resume the worn

patterns of lives interrupted,
closing ranks to cover up
a death. Love or whatever slopes
from afternoon to the drooping

shadows of an evening. More and more
we find attempts being made
to forget, but watch as a tottering world
bursts out of wood and seed.

35

Looking ahead to the first drive
uninhibited through lanes
and fields, how much of a revival
will we find? Swollen grain

will catch the sun, dart with swallows
and swifts. Hedgerows too
perhaps will shatter into flight, recall
centuries past. Slow

and easy should do the trick
and at least alleviate the fear
inside, the flashbacks. Verges will wake
herbs and cow parsley.

36

I can't stare over-long at the sun
as it daubs colour. The headaches
have resurfaced, drilling and stabbing the dawn
quiet. I wake like cicadas

crawling out. Your message helps
telling me it's not as warm
as it looks and there have been five helicopters
and planes already, the hum

of engines not yet so familiar
as to go without saying.
Perhaps a new relief. There will be pills
at the chemist's, waiting like daybreak.

37

I can never remember if it's tonight
that some of the front-doors
open for people to applaud. The sight
of life and connection withdraws

after a couple of minutes, vacating
the streets, leaving them to the police
and kids on motorbikes, but the gesture meets
others at least. The freeze

snaps, if only for a few seconds
and for the curious there's a chance
to see who is and isn't breaking,
how many are still dancing.

38

Seeing me growing stronger helps
to gild the time for you
and for me by reflection. Openings
suggest themselves, a few

hours out of the house, in the sun,
before the slanted golden evenings
of early autumn. Out in the country
the police would likely leave us

be and who'd know? Not yet
but by the end of May, perhaps,
when the verges are foaming at their sweetest
and whitest and the hedgerows are draped.

39

I look for signs of normality now
in the work you did yesterday
on the decking, music, the nods and bows
of giddy borders. As the tests

continue, I look for ways round
the probable eventual need
for me to leave the house behind,
if only to clear my head,

reboot. A stab at the lottery and the Pools
helps, not at all
like Mr Bleaney. Then your words call me
back from forgetting the world.

40

And now the honeysuckle buds
tease glimpses, sway
until the bedroom window could be
out at sea, a spray-flecked

reminder of crossings, making plans
for a life decades ahead
of our older now. Between the strands
of myth and memory, we decide,

commit. Soon they'll be sprung and bleeding
scent wherever we look,
them and the willowherb, greedy
for the gaps, riding their luck.

41

That we both mention how neatly
some poor sod
has had to fold the flags repeats
more than it knows. Loaded

terms and images stock up, from oak
panels, to the gestures, the failure
to convince. Before the virus he spoke out
in favour of the workhouse, nailed

his colours to the Victorian mast, this Deputy
PM. Now he tries
concern. You couldn't write it. We skip
the rest and keep our distance.

42

Another CD this morning
to remind me what has and does
inspire. Adding craft to abundance
I suppose, all those close

acoustic details, voices straight
from the field or the river. It's soothing
rather than recovery, lifted from the letters
in the porch or the hall, love

and disinfection. Always at its heart
though the same basic
connections so seldom found, art
as fresh as an untutored rose.

43

Was the music still going as you kicked
the windows out? The damp
rush of cold air rich
with clay, I remember, the stamp

stamp to give me room, the voices,
the two Dutch ladies
who stopped to help, followed by the noise
of metal as the fire-crew invaded

and lugged me out. But not the song
we had playing or when
it stopped. So hard to untangle
now from the mess at the scene.

44

Seeing past the lines brings us
that much closer. We reach
and touch hands, defy the lingering
catalogue of rules and restrictions,

continuing isolation. And meantime, increasingly,
my voice fits my words
once more. Favourite films appease
some of the quiet. Order

surrenders to order, to the most we make
of any time we can steal
and keep our own. The chrysalids are cracking.
I can hear them. The world is unpeeling.

45

Gardens respond to the sun, stretch
and swell. Footage emerges
of neighbours playing badminton with a hedge
for a net. Unless it's urgent

it has to wait. I'm wishing the pollen count
down in the hope you'll sleep,
losing myself to the steady want,
the vision of us slipping

clear. How many weeks now
since the crash? How long
for a bone to heal? I guess we'll know
when we know there's nothing wrong.

46

And the rhetoric goes on, the media drone,
the *fight*, the *front-line*. Veterans
of dead wars stand like bronze
cocks, their medals bright

and neat. Bowie was right, we're heroes
all. A woman wants
a parent's death awarded to the virus
instead, set and flaunted

in Portland stone. From here to Mons
and Tipperary the masons
are on the job, hammering honour
with the same old grace.

47

Unpoliceable, the tap tap
drip drip of pressure
sufficient to fell walls, the stopping out
a little longer, the tested

boundaries. Accident or design, it happens
given time. The valves
begin to seep, losing their grip
to those who forget themselves

as much as anything more. When we can
we'll drive together by cleaner
verge, hope my nerve stands
as the road bucks and leans.

48

The final adornment is one of my several
bandanas, worn higher
than I can remember, cowboy style, quivering
with every syllable and sigh,

lending my voice a smoker's husk
and gravity. We kiss freely
before you make the last adjustments
to the cloth, straighten my feet

and my jeans. Everything as it should be
and choices made, we pick up
close to where we left off, fool
no-one, slip our restrictions.

49

We pause at the front door, breathe
a world heady with scent,
wait as our eyes adjust, like leaves
to less cluttered light, the glint

and glare of cars and windows. Our glasses
blush protective tone
as the street, our street, rises
and resettles. And we move out, astonished,

taking the weather on our skin. The lurch
of my chair and your half-giggle
compete for attention with whole churchyards
of flowers, each birdcall triggered.

50

A tremor at first, barely to be distinguished
from the fluctuations of breath,
then a significant lurch, a jolt, bring
crashing home the gathering

life. It'll be what, another ten
weeks or so? The gender
we already know, as she clenches and unclenches
her cockleshell fists, distends

her liquid home. Come July,
come the rush, you'll cradle her
just as you cradled her mother
before, tearful and dismayed.

51

In visor and mask and overalls and gloves
he comes for me, for my blood,
as I lie half-awake, hovering
between worlds. I nod

rather than talk, keep my mouth
closed, as far as I can,
just in case, watch as he moves
around the bed, hands

fumbling at my arms, failing to find
a responsive vein. Then leaves
having brought the morning in,
with his rubbish as a parting gift.

52

Have they found him yet, I wonder,
whoever it is strolling
about as a plague doctor, outlandish
beak and all? Call it

what you will, but strictly speaking
is it even wrong? They're vaccine
trialling down at Oxford, tweaking
until their brains burst. Tracking

apps are coming soon. The pipers
and the papers call the tune
from the doormats of Edinburgh and Eyam.
The lab-rats and monkeys respond.

53

I'm sure they said ambulated,
the surgery, when they phoned,
as if it was the most natural
thing in the world. Only

it wouldn't be, not for me,
locked in the ward with you
locked out. And for what? To see
how long before the slow

fall? I'll take my chances, thanks,
split the time the way
we have and do, rather than hankering
for what we couldn't say.

54

We, the dark half of the bird-song
and the whispered word, remain
uncounted, pass mostly unheard
out of mind, mean

as much or less than discarded gloves
once we're done. Corridors
and wards ignore or forget as we're covered,
moved along, spared

the grim applause. And Johnson says
it hasn't happened, so
it hasn't. Hospitals are as safe as houses
and our graves are rose gardens.

55

The chirpy milkman, posed in wartime
rubble, resurrects,
brushes the dirt from his overalls, bares
his broken teeth. Creaking

like a fence in the wind, he'll knock and wait,
take two steps
backwards when someone appears and chatter,
sniffing out scraps

of news. Absent decades will do that
for you. He turns on a flapping
heel, whistles up the dead bluebirds
as if they were just asleep.

56

In Africa they dance the coffins home,
coordinate like starlings, brass
and drum. Add two-tone brogues and the sombre
disappears into jazz

and rhythm, carnival procession. Mourners
meet in their Sunday best,
resume where they left off or form
fresh acquaintance. Business

is sealed with a handshake or a word. Proceedings
over, the bearers leave
as one, rejoin those older dead
our paintings and friezes revive.

57

The biggest swarms there for seventy years
flutter and crawl, devour
miles of field. Farmland pares
down in a matter of hours.

Stubble rattles sticks in the drying
wind. Like snow drifts,
they cover and move on. Farmers try
flapping at them, beating the living

air, feel the hunger already
before it comes. And they'll grow
from what's being said, as the land bleeds
out and the rivers stop flowing.

58

However it's done, Bader clambers in,
completes the pre-flight checks,
takes to vacant skies, with that handsome
old Merlin speaking

volumes on the BBC. Or it's Churchill
puffing like a steam train
and his black dog panting and urgent
beside him, the soldiers and guns

he turned on Liverpool wiped out,
redacted. They're digging out the bunting
now, God help us, as the crippled
fighters come haunting in.

59

Reported cases in Paris slip
a month from January to December,
a little before you were having to sleep
on your front, with nebulisers steaming

every few hours. And how much
further here, attributed
to fever and flu, or unacknowledged
altogether, muted

and left to their own devices? We can ask
even if we find out
on the far side of never and their masks
resist the changing wind.

60

The same old story, the smirk
on official faces, as the graffiti
and harassment grow. Asian workers
have to take it, neither laugh

nor cry. Their kids have to dream the words
from their walls and doors,
sleep with fear. Stupid sordid
stuff, but always more

than enough to blind or convince, tease
our grossest instincts. Rumour
has it one poor guy had his eyes
slit on his way home.

61

With the garden centres edging
open now, or some of them
at least, you'll have your pick, imagine
how the profusion might assume

a preferred arrangement, bless the mornings
with colour, the sweet breath
of relief. And I can picture in turn
what it will mean to retrieve

normality from the tallies on the news, have bees
stumble in and out
between baskets and pots, messy
with pollen. Them and the butterflies.

62

My grandad never wore his gongs
from Burma or anywhere else
he was sent, barely said a word, belonging
instead to the brigade of tell them

nothing. And still the red arrows
split the London skyline
in perfect order, streets party,
ventilators sigh

as they fall and rise. And yet again
it's Vera bloody Lynn,
homemade bunting trembling on a string,
slurps of *Victory Gin*.

63

On the long tramp from Maharashtra
to Madhya Pradesh, following
the track, they slept. When the rush came
you'd like to think they felt it

only in their dreams. Police in khaki
sift through a scramble of belongings
and remains. Cleaners and construction workers
now denied a living

mingle in the wake of one of the few
trains left running,
their villages weeks off still. The confusion
sweetens the ripening sun.

64

Absolute consensus on state tv
among the most at risk,
happy it seems for life to start up
around them, while they kiss

the time goodbye. For how long though?
One with a rare condition
has given up on a wedding in October.
Another with a cancer wishes

on a vaccine. Each to their own, but the blackbird
sounds off from the hawthorn
regardless. And the hawk leaves a patch
of feathers to flutter on the lawn.

65

It even moves like a dog
on its four backward legs
as it patrols the grass and paths, flags up
warnings, pants. As regular

as clockwork soon in Singapore,
with its constant dorsal camera
unblinking, its inhuman voice in perfect
English. The sights aim

and assess. The voice insists on a safe
distance. Those on the benches
edge apart or stand up and drift
away from the sensors and the lenses.

66

It's when my head rests too long
against the head-board, I'm back
pressed up against the glass, hanging on
to your voice. The fear kicks in,

the tumbled black and light, the stretched
time waiting on someone, anyone
to come. Even the strange echo
and golden sky around us

as we slid and spun. And then it's gone
with the push of a button to raise
my head that little it needs to return me
to today's torn skies.

67

Our monthly anniversary passes
without the usual spree
of flowers. It's strictly funerals at the best
of the local shops, wreaths

and such. Not a regular wrap
or bouquet in sight, sadly.
So, I'm sorry, we'll have to tap
joy from our readymade

love, until it's business as usual
in the meadows. Or not sorry
as it happens, not remotely, the profusion
being all ours.

68

A cascade of petals from the makeshift houses
as speakers play hits
from the movies, police dance. A blaze
of life and colour fights

for attention against a backdrop of families
in a single room, bulldozed
shanties. Tartan bandanas lay claim
to a future between the folds

of khaki drill. House-calls are made
with birthday cakes for the young
and old. A Bollywood world parades
beneath its Indian sun.

69

I'm hoping you get lucky with the dentist
when you ring, luckier
than me with the GP, at least. It wants
sorting, that tooth, broken

or not. There's only so far
you can go on salt
and cloves, for sure. The cars and lorries
are back, I see, caught

between the cameras and the lights. It's right
what they say about toothache
being as hurtful as it gets. We fight it
together, grin, love on.

70

The phrase bobs up, like a reluctant burial
at sea, in message after
message. Our *new normal*, preparing
the way for what brave

other? Readjustment, hopefully
on more compassionate grounds,
a hands-free world, the scrape scraping
away of what we stand

or stood for? But for now, we keep
those cubic inches in our heads
and *what remains of us* remains the rippled
sunlight of love instead.

71

Above the Arctic, a rip mends
like water behind a stone
or moss on an abandoned car. Tender
kisses dare to want

more, first-time nervous. We could
couldn't we, soon? I'm wearing
the brand your kiss left me as the cold
reclaimed last night. My forehead

for now deemed safer than my lips
celebrates by not waking me
with the normal headache. Something to keep
in mind for the future as we make it.

72

They're killing prey-birds again, because
they can, cleansing estates
and uplands and lowlands for the guns and the grouse
and the glorious 12th. Kites

and peregrines drape like paper
bags, decorate hedgerows
until the wind or the ants or the leap
towards a context as yet

unscorched. Remember when we watched
from the Holy Cairn as the valley
mewed and filled with kites, spoke
the language of the rocks and the soil?

73

A series of initial tests are reporting
that the six rhesus macaques
have responded well. Some way short
of a miracle cure, but attractive

click-bait nonetheless. Viral loads
reduced, antibodies
flourishing within a month, in the hunt for good
news, they give the studies

that shot they need. Deflated markets
wait to pile in. The waves
and canals of idle towns sparkle
so blue that we miss any shivers.

74

We click from one vehicle to the next
looking to shake the mud
and broken metal from our minds, protect
ourselves against the flood

of images. Fail. Try breathing
out. Let it all
go. Whatever else we retrieve
from the wreckage, we have to call

time on the shudder inside. It'll be
the wet roads that get to me,
I know, the loss of control, the trees,
lorries, light's uneasiness.

75

Rego dancers flap and stoop,
pick an insect or a frog
from riverside grass. A snapped loop
closes around the ragged

bundle of twigs in a Sussex tree,
hatchlings in fragments of shell
and dust, the first young we've seen
as far as we can tell

since the oldest of the oaks left standing
sprung. They tried last year
too, it seems, but as things can,
the moment and the season passed.

76

By night the cathedrals and St George's Hall
are rainbow-lit for the cancelled
parade. The sandstone answers, appeals
both to the future and our penchant

for nostalgia. Cavafy was here
a while, stood out like
a lone tree at the heart of a spare
field. Or as an outlandish joke,

a walk on waiting for the next period
drama, when the film-crews
return. Silver gulls appear
and veer away with their screams.

77

We can take our bucket-lists to the sea
and drown our sorrows there,
where the sailors and soldiers are free
as waves to sing *we're here*

because we're nowhere else. Shell-holes
and sumps and rock-pools turn
to lead in an evening sun. Shallow
graves never learn

more than that they were dug. Ancestors
leave the Menin Gate
to the bugles, saunter our way on an insistent
haar, remember to matter.

78

Whenever we eat it's never just food
any more than that cloud-burst
was just weather. I've given up on it fading
now, hoping instead

that it might merge into one of our sunsets
without infecting those memories
too. The golden light haunts me
like the living dreams and limbos

of my hospital days. But not with you
here to make me laugh
it down. The mind's a flower, a new
flower, a now and a hereafter.

79

Less than enamoured of my plan to head
to matches kitted out
in a vampire mask, if indeed
I'm ever allowed to shout

myself dizzy from the stands again,
you work your way through
the consignment of stock we've been sent,
emerge in a visor, a new

mask, for all the world like Hoffman
in *Outbreak*, or a *Quatermass*
scientist, kiss me, mouth to mouth,
from the far side of the plastic.

80

It's of a night the Rebel Bear quits
his cave in the mountains, lugging
his sprays down to Bath Street.
A man in monochrome drags

a virus ball and chain, the virus
in leaf green. And on a white wall
in the west end, lovers snog, daring
the dark to come. Hauled

aside, their masks are the lapsed bluebells
of a dud spring, flags
gifted to a cutting wind, queues
and borders and eloquent gags.

81

The first traffic jam in a while
interrupts your journey
here, catches the sun on millpond
glass. Ozone warnings

resurface. It's evening before we settle
fully into our calm. You present me
with pictures of a glistening beach, sheets
like the first snow, a view

from reclining loungers, with, I think,
next year in mind,
a green island between a ring
of reefs, an easy wind.

82

I'll not deny it. Given a chance
shielding or no shielding
likely enough I'd be one of those dancing
with the reaper around the fields

of Anfield Road, losing it
when the title comes
home. As always you get the difference
the risk makes. To be somewhere,

anywhere, seems good to me,
to feel the blood flexing,
to be pushing aside the dead leaves
and the dirt, to be hoping and expecting.

83

A groundswell of song carries from the garden
and Derrycairn, buries
any thought else. Wordless
clusters of sound flurry

and dip, repeat their appeal, invent
and extemporise. A blackbird
fills the pre-dark, answers and sends out
its spiralling call. It's immaculate

for the half hour it takes to merge into the sunset
behind the hawthorn bushes
and the churchyards, the names and the mossy stones,
the wake and its impending hush.

84

Not before time, footpaths
brush and bristle gorse
and balsam. All the way to the water
birds alarm and chorus,

shatter the calm, encourage that ideal
of a marina or a flash left
almost entirely to us. A feeling,
a vision, and as yet aloof

from the real. But with room enough
for mosaic wings and staggered
flight to hint recovery, brevity,
a future past the nettled tracks.

85

Unbroken voices, flecked with age,
ring more true now
than ever, quaking with their rage
or passion, staring down

the barrel. Think Heaney in the ambulance
with love in mind, Abse
keeping on, or George Malone, with the game up
but having a final stab

at standing to watch the Liverpool docks
revive, the dead space
fill with shouts and horses, unlocked
and acquiring an unlikely grace.

86

Having been in lockdown and shielding
at Windsor, it's on *Balmoral Fern*
she rides out, a fell pony yielding
at each tweak, burning

in the sun and glistening like a coal seam
shown the light. Tweed
jacket and a pair of jodhpurs, assembly
completed by a headscarf, she threads

a path between young and distanced trees.
And the lenses respond, as they do,
twitchers training on the hint, the tease
of a rare gull, a dodo.

87

Jadon Sancho hoists up his yellow
jersey, celebrates
the first of three well-taken goals
at Paderborn. The weight

of a conscience screams *Justice for George
Floyd* on his under-shirt.
American streets burn and marchers
gather in London. The hurt

ripples out from the White House
lawn and keeps going
through the grain of old newsreel, hoses,
batons, the living and the lost.

88

That we can even discuss colour schemes
for my new chair speaks
volumes, with us thinking along similar
lines especially. Equals

in everything, I can rely on us choosing
much the same and living
with the glut of associations loosened
in the process, the heather

and gorse we didn't get to see,
the waters off Mull. Like the weavers
do when they work their world into the tweed
between the lulls and the waves.

89

When the reunion comes it's as a wave
of pent respect and love,
mother to son, son to mother,
a hug, an admission of having

missed one another, brave
and pure. Small wonder
your voice cracks and your tears unravel
in the telling. The mending of sundered

bonds has that simple beauty
about it, unashamed
for all his being a man now, rooted
in the pain and happiness we become.

90

This throat of mine could be a cooling board
worse. Ask Skip James
and old Son House what they heard
on the Delta. We're cotton ripe

for the picking, the sharecropper's meagre
yield, except in this case
it's nothing lasting, nothing of intrigue
a restful night won't replace

with relative peace. The letters can wait
before they're hammered home.
The copper slides and rusting resonator
guitars can sing out the summer.

91

So we go *Ruby Red* for the chair
having made the same choice
together and apart. The depth and warmth
channel our decades of noise,

the floodlit dramas, the times you've raised
my left arm to salute
shattered defences, the delirious haze
of a late winner, as remote

as gull-screams to life past the stands
and the burger vans. Sunsets
too, driving west with the windscreen
drinking it all in.

92

Ambarnaya river encrimsons with oil
from the power plant at Norilsk,
the pillars supporting one of the fuel tanks
having sunk. Red milk

as opposed to blood and apocalypse
but filling a hundred odd
square miles as the pollutant rips
a path through the mottled

frost. Alaska, the *Exxon Valdez*,
Greenpeace, suffocated
lungs and gills, blank eyes
return to haunt us from the water.

93

It's abattoir-sweet in the sun
when the removal vans park up
in Corona, New York. And there they'll stand
until they're filled, start up,

drive on. A regular procession to
and from the parlour and the undertaker
past coping, doing his best.
But how do you keep track

when there's no end in sight? Wrapped
in anonymous white and placed
line by line, it never stops
and the vans come every day.

94

Our private consensus speaks in favour
of caution, doubling down
on my bandana obsession, as the protests gather
like geese at the margins and stones

splinter the windows. And who can blame
them, when the brutal loop
of official murder continues to claim
its victims? It seems hope

lives only in the songs and in our promise
to live every minute
to the full, to make a future, a home
of the mess, to draw a line.

95

Within a shout of the cliffs and the tombstoners
fished injured from the waves,
seahorses interrogate the seagrass, clumsy
elegant, as green as gravesides

and lazy rivers. Divers keep the score,
identify a good sixteen
on one dive alone, as rare
as a virgin birth wriggling

through the Dorset tide, including juveniles
and pregnant males. As the boats
dither in their moorings, snouts hoover up,
neither swim nor float.

96

Winston and Julia confront the photos
of their fuckfest in the forest
and in their quaint apartment. For each thoughtless
glory there's a sordid

memento in black and white, time
underneath the constant
lights. For her it's no more a crime
than any other flaunted

for the cameras and the public hangings. For him
it is or was a rebellion
of the mind, a vision and a dream
rectified and then blown to hell.

97

No retraction, as yet, of that statement
from the BMA
scrubbing the principle of human rights
for those of us swaying

the wrong side of the general good.
No mention since, hardly,
past our private unease. If there's a road
back it remains cordoned off

by the tremble of official tape. God
help us, or no-one will
unless they change their mind, a wink and a nod
and all boxes filled.

98

We'll take it as it comes this year,
mark and celebrate
our seven years and longer married
and together as a moment and a gateway

to more. Whatever form we give
the day, it means turning
inwards, focussing on us and on living
partly as we have, while learning

from the sway of recent circumstance,
balancing on a wire or the wall-tops
you braved as a girl, gymnast and dancer,
never a thought of falling.

99

They're selling masks at the club shop
with the Liverbird perched
over stifled breath, cropped
from the pair by the river and the resurgent

docks. Black or red or both
in a pack of four, with the bird
in gold, hanging its wings on the weather
and our ifs and whens. Ignored

or revered, the unavoidable suggestion
is indefinite resumption, a rising
unscorched from inferno and coming to rest
between our shifting skies.

100

Now that the bees are back among the crevices
of the pondside wall, the borders
are not what you'd call *loud* with them,
but busy enough for their orderly

processions to bless our garden-time
as it comes. My gran spoke
to her bees, gave them the news, same as
taking the latest to her slumbering

stone at the crem, but with an agenda of ensuring
they'd stick around. We'll take pictures,
pin the different types to words
and drawings, minute particulars.

101

This is where it gets tricky
as restrictions ease, beaches
flock with weekend travellers, stadiums
and turnstiles start to creak

open. Life's always been a game
of risk and reward though, for us
at least, a case of ignoring the flimsiness
of it all and cranking up the music.

Even so, the future is written
in sand. A bomb still ticks
and crackles in my head. The old brittleness
inside strobes and flickers.

102

The gravitas of Burton's voice hisses
out of time, repeats
the warning of our being watched, visited
by superior minds. A neat

halo glows leaf-green
around Mars. Light
and Oxygen in a serene tryst, as seen
from an orbiter, admit

the possibility of holidays there
breathing a kind of conditioned
air, seeing earth almost as a star
or a neglected and nagging ambition.

103

Cardboard cut-outs of the living and the dead
watch from a corner of the Amex
as Brighton win at home. There's crowd-noise,
or not, canned like the theme-song

of a non-existent film, the bassline
provided by the ghost of a gutted
whale. I go with *off*, replace
the lot with the touchlines, the neutral

grounds watching Liverpool reserves,
Anfield, Southport, wherever,
and a glimpse of the next *Great* surfacing,
the told you so of discovery.

104

A few drops of rain from the tailgate
and branches as we wait in the carpark
for the doctor, mask-up, grateful to be called
from the nowhere much. No wards

and corridors. A curtained section of the common
room instead, serves
for a theatre. A breeze from the doors, a presumption
of relative safety, careful

preparation, with me trying not
to speak. Then back to us
and the fallowing as the fields and the verges clot
with flowers and their repercussions.

SHIELDING

Something is broken somewhere
not that we heard the quiet
snap. The jokes stop
short of this, the latest coming in
from Madrid, a doctor gritting
his teeth, compelled to report
the snuffing out of hope,
elderly and vulnerable shortened,

deliberately sedated. Worse
even than the denial of care
is the killing, the writing off
of so many of us, that unspoken curse
in nervous looks. It was there
for sure at the hospital when we spent
twenty-seven hours with me hovering
on a trolley. And when they meant me

to stay there, a curtain-swish
from their fresh admission, a possible
virus case coughing
like a sandstorm. Now I'm leashed
to the safe-side of the view, housebound
and shielding. Days slide past
in soft focus. Love
waits on your next visits.

SOMEPLACE

Another morning slides across the glass
and death has slipped behind the news.
For now, I watch the weather passing
instead, the green confusions
of bark and leaf, the loosened stars

of honeysuckle, tested, teased, by clean
and eager breeze. The thought of us
arriving at a billowed keening
shoreline somewhere refuses
to leave me be today. The sheen

of sea-light hovers just beyond the trees
and rooftops, intercedes between
earth and sky. And if there's a place free
from all that fear, it's leaning
out and away, where the gulls wheel

and stray, the tankers stretch and disappear
behind their new horizons. Opt
for back-road quiet and steer well clear
of the lens, and we'll open
worlds again, resume, re-explore,

more aware of what it means to have time
aside. A field of windmills rolls
over angled shadows. One becomes
another becoming all
I want the day to be or seem.

FOXES

Your late-night drive again
pauses to watch them change
the road, cross at an angle
to the world. The second
night in a row, with the danger
seemingly checked

and dismissed. When you write
they pad clear of the lights
and bins, the tested litter,
fill the room
here with themselves, admit
that edge of something

more than lockdown. For now
they thrive, play, show off
in the void, content to allow us
these glimpses, but never
quite become exposed
or familiar, give us

only what they can take back
when the time comes. The cracks
ease. They slip the fractures,
move between us,
continue along their tracks
with the night redefined.

SEVENTH ANNIVERSARY

June appears to have been chosen
as the point when our clenched and closed
world can throw off at least some
of the shackles. Not that they've said,
but it's all there for the reading
when we're ready. And summer

is always more than that for us
of course, never far from the *yes*
and the *yes* returned, the rose
gold and the kiss. And will be soon
again as we rest like sunglow
on a stone wall, not just close

but closer even than when doves
bolted through the shifting weather,
took us with them to the next
horizon. Or the singer poured
our song into the cool air, word
for word. Here or in breaking

fresh ground, we build each year on years
past. But this anniversary
with the car crash and all, life
has to truly shine and each chance
we get to make our shared time dance
we'll take, answer, believe in.

OWL IN LOCKDOWN

A vacant road allows you to slow
to the same loping pace. You follow,
careful not to spook the hunting ghost
or topple the balance. A white rose
by moon and starshine, or foam rolling

in and under on a void shore. Words
aim and miss, leaving you and the gift
of contact, the extraordinary
floating somewhere between distinct worlds,
listening and homing in, sifting

verge and uncropped grass. In the half-dark
you belong more than ever, released
to be both bird and shadow, grafted
onto the living dream. The rift-land
blinks, shivers in a hint of sprung breeze.

PAST THE TREELINE

Days like these I can't help looking
for more than the window-view of sparkling
trees. I can't help hoping for open
roads, for you to pull up on the sloping
drive, breeze in, make remarkable
what would otherwise be a luckless

day. Whatever, there's a place,
a dimension, in which you're already here.
Isn't that how the theory goes?
dragging us with it to the forests and lost
lanes. Suits me, all that shared
green, sun on our skin, amazed

streams and shorelines, before the roads
clog again. Taking our chances
with the law too has its tasty side,
bracing as the turbines roll and the tide
claws back at the shingle. It all stands
for something, I suppose. There's a wood

not far off, reeking garlic, bound to be,
unless the garlic's gone by now.
I never can keep up. If not today
then soon, yes? The distance will play
havoc with your mind if you let it. I know.
I can feel it, hear it, calling through the trees.

BEFORE YOU FLY HOME — GOA

Your last days there this time around
fittingly involve the softness
of beach, the gush
and hiss of wave-end,
the white heat. Time in accordance
with the expanding
and contracting
shadows allows you to relax

out of or into yourself, grow
with the moment. Life will catch up
at some point. Boats
will leave their tracks, slide
across the view. The Jeep will come
to pick you up. Beach
will become road
and runway. Sea becomes the miles

home. For now though, it is present
tense only, the sun on your face,
bird-chatter, light
tripping on the web
of ripples, the need to find shade
or take to the throb
of water. Sleep
comes and goes, offers fresh visions

perhaps of us, either right there
or somewhere else. Your planes move on
as separate
thoughts, carrying you
nearer, little by little. Coasts
change and become new
themes. The door clicks
open. You taste of distance closed.

FROM POST-OP TO THE WARD

I recognise my voice again
by the time you join me
under the lights. You reclaim me
with a kiss as the staff

unmask, relax into private
conversation. We sync
almost to the minute, make light
of my time folded deep

under. I wake. You walk in, lean
over me. Or it feels
and stays that way, even weeks on,
in my head. The rest blurs

into the general process
of doors, lifts, Southport pier
stretched across a wall. Back to us
on the ward, making sense

of the difference, the wound hushed
by a wad of dressings,
part of us now. Until it heals
and we can love the scar.

KINGFISHER

Dressing has to be so careful
even months on, with my arm like glass
and my head still a potential disaster
zone. Tops with room to spare,
loose jumpers, forgive what I can't
forget, yield as it's all done
with kid gloves. The day slips
from behind its early haze, sparkles
then fades. Nothing all that remarkable,
but better than yesterday perhaps. Skip

forward and your message postpones tonight
with the promise of better to come. A course
instead, a kingfisher cake, sure
to be every bit as good, as bright
and beautiful as your best, but online
this time, rather than in the confines
of a studio. And it'll do you good, kindle
or rekindle the girl who could pass
hours with her crayons, curled on the grass,
making rainbows begin and end

between perfect houses and a swollen
sun. The dressing, the getting up
can wait. Or I can let it happen
anyway, with an eye on the great unfolding
when, if, it ever comes.
And on us training your binoculars on the brambles
and branches beside some river,
hoping on the swoop and recovery, the flash
meaning more than daylight and rushes,
responsive circles of dark and silver.

KICKING IN

Here today or not, it's still you
and the moment we knew dominating
the meander of thoughtless thought. I'm late
with my message today and no excuses
other than the need to write with more
than the not much of morning. We're there though

always, wherever there happens to be
this time. You'll be looking after your mum,
making sure she eats, has something
to get her through the day. I can see you
from here as you coax her outside into the garden,
share with her the cascade of starlings

clamouring for their feed. And when you write
in one of the gaps between so much else
it'll be the same blessing, the same breeze
sweeping away the dregs of a night
that broke a little early for my liking
and it'll be the same tenderness kicking in.

EID AL-FITR AT THE MARTHA LUTHERAN CHURCH

Worshippers gather, keep their distance,
offer their prayers, observing masked up
deference. Ramadan restrictions
end in the filtered light and glowing
windows of Kreuzberg's church, the Neuköln
mosque having only so much mat-space

now. Both the Pastor and the Imam
share their concerns, their hopes for something
better. With sunset poised, the same air
listens or not, depending. Pictures,
instruments, decorate the church-walls,
vanish as *salat* swells between them.

FAR SHORE

I write to tell you
I wouldn't want you driving
in this, as fresh gusts
rattle at the doors, windows
catch the flicks of whipping stems.

And it's true. The fear,
the flashbacks fill any space
I leave open. Life
stutters. Music or the balm
of certain nature docs helps.

Aldridge and Goldsmith
singing with the dawn chorus,
then leaving the last
notes to the birds. The tender
steel of Gaughan or Christy Moore.

Most of all you, us,
on the far shore of all this
hurt. That time we stopped
off at Lomond, warmed ourselves
on unlikely winter sun.

It's all there somewhere,
suspended, waiting to be
revisited, found
and explored over, enjoyed
like our post lock-down kisses.

MAIDEN FLIGHT

Bothered trees respond to give
and take, blustered and bending
with it, rain-fresh. Tomorrow lives
large in our minds, the lanes
past the sunflower farm, the drive,
hopefully less on edge
than I feel right now. It's drawn
with the lightest and most skittish of hands,
all of it, balanced where ridge

meets sun and open sky.
The latest shower is hung-out and drying.

Call it my maiden and fledgling
flight, as we lean with the pitch of bends,
remember that lit kestrel, like a wound
or a fern-leaf, a moment etched
into the surface of another drive
the same way. That it's mapped and planned
ahead of time relieves
a little, perhaps, like your hand
on mine nails our shared belief.

SHORELINE SAPPHIC

Seeing us as part of a shimmer glowing
past the moment, finding a way to step out
into what we make of the future, takes on
edge with an email

fresh in, seeking help for a young man, student,
injured, just as life was about to open,
sounds like either 5 or a 4, the fracture.
Nothing as yet on

how it happened. Yes, I'll be writing, soon as,
saying what I can, but it's always us there,
shining through, regardless, and us that anchors,
like those encrusted

iron men, at odds to the tide, where Crosby's
sandscape stretches out. We'll be back, embracing
sea-breeze when we can, no agenda, pared down,
taking our face-on

stand against whatever the weather brings on,
hope, belief and all that as givens. Granted,
carving somewhere out of the limbo, breaking
waves as they roll in,

never comes as easily as the distanced
tankers make it seem, but we'll manage. Breathe it
softly, arms around me, and let it happen,
halves of a constant,

dark and light, the lull in a shell-hole, frame it
any way you like. It's the contact matters,
calling out of hollowing wrecks with love-song
shanties and kelp-smack.

SHORESIDE

You breeze in and the worry
disappears. It really does,
as readily and neatly
as new petals and the noise

in my head falls calm. I'm there
on our shoreline, with the last
of the light on the wave-ends
and the give and take of grass

on the dunes. We watch as gulls
catch the fall and rise, mewing
and then fading, giving way
to stars. Staying wrapped in you

opens such wide horizons.
The soft hiss of ebbing tides
throbs, pulses and carries us
clear, as far off as we need.

A BLACKBIRD AMONG THE BERRIES

A blackbird returns for more of the berries
on the shrubs hanging over
from the garden next door. The whirs
and clicks of birdsong have been smothered
now for a while, what with the weird
weather and all. There's movement
among the stems, but not much
beyond an occasional rush

followed by more inertia. I'm still
sweating like a dockyard horse
for no reason I can think of. I can feel it
running its quiet course,
taste the salt in the little rills
now and then. Worse things
happen at sea, amid other washed up
sayings. I wish I could see past these bushes

to the wide open, the working estuaries
and shorelines within earshot of the stands,
the cathedrals announcing themselves to early
hints of sun. Wonders
never cease. There are dolphins in the Mersey,
or so I've heard. Abandoned
ground comes back to life given
time. I know you're doing everything

you can to get things ready for me
again. Neither of us
would have planned it quite this way
of course, as this hollowed house
slides towards yours. What can I say though
that I haven't said? There are clusters
of berries and that blackbird in the soft give
and take of stems and dolphins in the river.

POEMS FROM TRANSITIONS

I   *A breath*

I hold the machine's gift
of breath, let its softness
lift us clear, hovering
over the thought
before it's lost to the difference
between light and water.

We're a kiss of sun on a wing
beat, the stray song
caught and carried from a tangle
of albums played
thin, the chance exchange
of what never fades.

We settle where we land,
feathering beaches, lending
both the deliberate and the random
more than they lack
to become a part of our landscape
of healing fractures.

And then the fragile pressure
we keep our own, measureless,
increasingly sharp and precious,
detached from its time
and always past resistance
as our breath climbs.

2   *Final*

June crackles outside
gasping windows. The warm-up
mats are basking, stretched

at the fringe of those
where, in a few more minutes,
we'll meet. I stretch, tweak

every muscle
and joint, ease them out, breathing
mountains and the rush

of young streams. The crowds
lean in from their world, become
that chattering leaves

create from air
and drift, ripples extending
past the time's hidden

horizon. His name
and mine share the microphone
with applause. We step

out of our selves, watched
by that other eye somewhere
above. *Be first. Grip*

hard. Move. The mantra
is a prayer-flag now, sparks
of cherry blossom

broadcasting spring. *Be
first. Grip Hard. Move.* Balance breaks
and resettles, shifts

through gears and levers,
works an opening, suggests
and then refuses,

catches a moment
off-guard. The scoreboard flashes
a signal, counts down

to the last word, stops
at the referee's raised arm,
the bow, the handshake.

4   *Resurrection of the Untermenschen*

A metal door creaks apart
releasing bleary-eyed survivors,
those who can, assisting those
who can't negotiate the smart
drop from van to road. They lift
the wheelchairs, placing them as close
as possible to the side, cough
the gas from burning lungs. They move

with dreamlike softness, understanding
masked by faces locked in riddles
the doctors and the soldiers fail
to solve. The scene escapes the guns
and leads them clear of compounds, slides
towards the point where borders fall

open. And not just here, but miles
away behind discreet and smiling

towns, woodlands shivering seas
of birch. The same reversal catches
on, bequeaths a sense of what
now? Reporters wait, their questions
cocked, trying to gaze between the cracks
in what they thought they knew. Throats
gulp from bottles and canteens offered
more in the name of disbelief

than love. They'll take it though and drift
somewhere off the radar, live
outside of rules, breathe thankful
and unforgiving, never forget the shaft
of angry light, engines dithering
to a halt. They'll eat, laugh, drink
themselves daft, have kids and meet up
sometimes once the dust settles.

5   *At home among flowers*

As if all those holes
still yawning on Google Maps
have meadowed over
into vertical summer,
troughs ride the walls, baskets

balance by the door
and take up corners, bees nest
and cosy outside
bedroom windows, all part of
the vision you've kept vivid

waiting for that day
when I roll up, find a way
to carry you in
past the threshold on my knee,
or we make it up, make up

for it in other ways,
leave the bi-folding doors wide,
breathing it all back
in to the point where we'll lie
for hours without moving.

7   *Return journey*

We carve the night a path
between regular
angles of aged stone
and wavering mist.

Leaning west, with Sheffield
half an hour
behind, the picturesque
of our outward drive

returns by huddled slabs
and towers, breathy
trees. A rock or stump
in the road shivers

life, hunches wings,
stares with question
marks for eyes. Slowing,
we turn on instinct,

circle back to the point,
only to find
the watcher gone. We decide
it must have been

obsessing over prey,
delete the thought
of any hurt to the bird,
prefer to leave it

out there somewhere
the headlights miss.

8   *Two chairs in Goa*

Captured against the mauve ripples
the two chairs are ours to complete
any time, poised
between wishes left
open for us, and the sun's last
flourish. Our hands mesh
endurance, hold
the thought on which so much depends

for us. Our voices blend with those
of morning and evening boats
never caught out
by sudden changes,
or any difference more than
the next wave. Answers
forget questions
ever mattered here. We can sip

long glasses, tilt ice, balance lights
at a distance from their harbours
and hotels. Birds
have never felt more
like separated souls. Dust turns
everything else
its own colour
as we watch, learning the patience

of the hoofed gods. They make their way
down to the sand, settle knowing
their own safety
like their horned shadows
has a rhythm lost on the world
beyond. The two chairs
take us out past
the point where our patterns converge.

PICTURED — YOU HOLDING YOUR DAD'S HAND

The fingers of your left hand
take the weight of his right, mend,
and nurture. So hard to see
this and be unmoved. You blend

into your shared time. The clock
stops for the photo, then ticks
over from early morning
to the sunlit room, the shock

of his leaving. We live this
over and over, listen
for the change of breath, the long
pause. Love brings us back to his

example of what it means
to care, to be cared for. Sense
struggles against the cold fact
and comes back to tenderness

communicating in hushed
terms, what seems to be a bruise
spreading on his skin. You knew,
always do somehow, more used

than most to the marginal
changes and the convergence
of physical signs. The weeks
you spent sleeping right there merge

with collections of childhood
images, your running wild
in a simpler world. You hold
and keep holding him, both still

and sharing the precious hours
with an acute awareness
of what was to come. Two hands
rest like landscapes, or two birds.

YOU'RE HERE

You come in and open up
the room, cope so readily
with everything we've got
on our plates. And I need that

elevation so much today
with the shadows on the scan
after my dad's tests. You toughed
and you loved it out, held hands

with your dad the whole way through
to the slowed time of that late
August afternoon. You did
what you could and more, waited

beside him, slept in his room,
kept the human side of pain
alive for him, found his smile
with a film, one of those tunes

he loved. That poem you wrote
and read out loud with the church
hanging on each word, returns,
and the churning of so much

emotion you bit down on
throughout. Now you're here, you're proof
against the dark, survival,
that spark life catches from love.

LOVE ISLAND

So, next time, when we're killing
time with *Love Island*
you'll know not to over-fill
the gap left by my idle
question with a list of those silver-tongued
egos, strutting their smiles

across the screen. For future reference
the proper answer, when asked
who you fancy, isn't several
dozen of the contestants, basking
on the loungers. Just imagine I'd given
you that response, asking

for trouble, I know, but suppose I did,
that beautiful dangerous light
would be back in your eyes, wild
for the first excuse to ignite,
daring me to say it again, middle-ground
nowhere to be found. We admit it

giggling over the thought. As if,
right? And yet, there
you go, with your whoever they are, thriving
on ideals I had carved
into my own muscles once, a lifetime
since, for all our laughing.

TRIBUTE
(David Bowie Night)

A pout and a kiss grace the mirror
with the stage calling. The last flourishes
fuse scarlet lightning to the cheek-bones
made immaculate by his surgeries,

confirming tonight's transformation
as his best yet. His chest was shaved
this morning, as soon as he caught
the news. Mortal after all, average

in that at least. But it's an ill
wind. The phone was bound to ring, fill
a couple of the blank nights. People
just can't help it. They have to feel

something, theirs or not. On the radio
driving down it was the same greedy
pathos all the way, the predictable
standards picking the bones, parading

patches of the collective grief
with barely a break for ads. Reverence
increases face to face with the finished
product. Shining back, any difference

from his album covers evaporates
to the space between stars. Escaping
the green room's coffee-smell, he clears
his throat, hears the dark static snapping.

All those zeros impress with their blank eyes
collecting tropes as they go, Spanish goats,
the wrought iron, almost elegant

above the railway lines and gates. And the bodies
of course, bulldozed into heaps, as if life
had never tickled in their lungs, lit their eyes

for more than their last seconds. It all adds up
to the same great hollow. Words repeat

themselves, understand only that this
happened. The small towns, cities even, stand
apart, some of them, gather tourists,

grin or gape for photographs. Others are just clearings
between trees. That myth about the birds

not singing tells us more about the listener
than the birds. There are voices, always,
lost in their pain, perhaps, but still there for the hearing

should we try. Unpeel us, take us back
past the point where it all began
to be more than ideas. Lives begin over, become music,

dances waiting to be excused. Houses return to meals
and snaking candles. Prayers answer themselves
and love remembers half-forgotten names,

re-learns their shape on its lips and tongue. Numbers,
tattoos, like oven doors, finally start to lose
count. Not entirely, of course, but just enough.

RUTH DORFMANN BY SAMUEL WILLENBERG

How long? in educated Polish.
Her hair parts, tumbles away
from the delicate skull. Her words stay
hovering, even as an engine rolls

once she's gone, a Russian tank
taken in battle. Others follow
the same path and keep following
all day, interrupted by the tank

again churning over. In bronze
she's liquid, pliant, the same knowing
girl who wished her barber a low
farewell, and let him go. His response,

Ten minutes, her name, *Ruth
Dorfmann*, share the calm around her
bowed head. She sits alone
half-shaved as the sky moves.

REMEMBRANCE DAY SEQUENCE

I   *A shell falls*

(Edward Thomas at Arras)

And with it swipes the breath from lungs
accustomed more to gentle burn
of exercise, the subtle turn
away from winter into spring.

Or else a bullet smashing through
the niceties of shell, the thump
of carpet battered clean, the slumped
response, as if he almost knew.

But didn't quite, until the heave
of sky, an angled slab of trench
at odds with what it was. The wrench
resettles, either way. Dust lifts.

A shattering of birds retrieves
abortive hedgerows, dead-end tracks
between his erstwhile fields. And back
to quivered ash, his call leaving

love behind for the fertile stretch,
Arras splintered, a wasted match.

(Ivor Gurney by the water)

There's one presents him looking out
across a sheet of water, hand,
protecting from the glare, branded
mind and eyes. At a distance shouts

and moans, the music of dulling
guns, carry on a sweetened breeze,
collecting tenderness. Teased free
from days, when discipline of drill

was punctuated by the warmth
of accents fresh from home, a calm
returns. And with it Gloucester, charmed
from OS Maps and friends. A swarm

of fragments shifts through makeshift graves
and gas in lilac blooms. The din
of hives. Before that open sheen
obliterating with its give

and take of wave, reduces life
to wards, replaces grief with grief.

3   *Death-bed*

(My grandad in hospital)

You know when something makes you smile
despite yourself? For all the cloy
of morphine breath, I grin, allow,
indulge, the change of mood to steal

from mortars puffing men away
beside him. Never more than drink
and dreams before, the jungle brings
them back, admits to more than hazed

evasions. Digging must have helped
as well, the runner beans, iron
tang of soil on his hands and shirt,
the soil besmirching his lapels

and shoes, the matching demob strides
or wedding suit. His love of those
with whom he stood, he's never lost.
His admiration too. Or pride

at having fought with Gurkhas. Hurt
though, when my gawky smile bursts out.

4   *Medic*

(Razan Al Najjar, Gaza)

Within sight of razor wire
she moves, a butterfly, dance
and dancer, under hail and glance
of bullet. Canisters of tear

gas confuse established lines
and definitions. Somewhere close
a sniper slides his glass across,
selects his target, both pinning

down and letting go, as the mood
allows. Then finds the girl he wants.
The rest we know, the blood flaunting
white, her medic's coat intruded

on, the headlines. Words survive her
expressing what it is to live
for others, fight for her belief
in who and where she is. The drive

by ambulance does nothing more
than bring her back to be confirmed.

5   *Death of a homeless soldier*

(Darren Greenfield, Edinburgh)

A fixture in his uniform
outside the station. Cardboard sign
displays service number, finished
with a blessing, the basic terms

of a plea for help. Back-story
links him with both a private school
and Bosnia, years of holding
out for something more than soft words,

lip-service. At a loss, but part
of routine days for those who pause
or carry on. Attempts to close
him in, rehouse him, only brought

another dose of those routines
he thought he'd left between the dust
and toppled walls. Infection plus
a stroke at forty-seven. Thin

as glass. Cheek-bones poking through him.
Half a page or so in the news.

LETTER FROM A PRIVATE, DUNKIRK

An accompanying snap is that paradox
of weathering and youth
smiling, half smiling,
from eighty years
back. The skin and uniform
having gradually assumed
the same evening yellow,
a faded primrose, tell us
some of what aloof
and censored words miss. Bluff,

of course, the letter, or parts of it,
at a guess, with talk
of victory to be cheaply won
early in the war, the certainty
of returning home, and far from
imagining his name carved
into the village memorial, just
beneath the cross. A lustre
about it, too, though awkward
in hindsight, given it was likely scrawled

on the run, before it was abandoned,
along with plenty more,
near Dunkirk. Found
by a German soldier, handed in
at the appropriate embassy, it gets home
in its own time, somehow,
to those of his relatives alive
and anything but living
in the vaguest hope of hearing
from a brother as remote as the highest birds.

THE SHARK-SINGER

He sings to the spirit inside the shark
and generations for whom the same song
has brought its reunions hungering
up to the dug-out boats. Wordless, the dark

and sun of flickering rhythms, sparkled
webs of light, the chant reaches, belonging
deeper than his eyes know, honing its long
note for the hours and days it takes to start

the dance. An interest begins to find
an answer, tracking molecular change
to the sea-shell rattle in his hand, flecks

of blood. Noosed, it thrashes to a mindless
trance, suspended under a float, hanging
between the singer's lifetime and the next.

BACKWASH PARADE

(after the picture by Valerie Ganz)

A shower-scene in which men drown
as much of their work as they can
leaves its mark somewhere
deep. Voices rumble
up assumptions, the sound

of wheels catching on a moment
out of kilter, dust coming home
to roost on decades
since. A few seconds
of heat streaks the tiles, numbs

a scouring blast. A row of globes
flickers light among those scrubbing
each other's bodies,
making their huddle
make sense. Model pits, jobs

worth the trudge from dark to darker
worlds, compete. Or struggle harder
to make themselves known
above what glares down
on their stone-baulked towns. Words

grab what they can, remember clouds
and beer, anything they can hold
onto. Weekends off
maybe, with their coughs
not recovered, but dulled

a little by pit swimming-pools
and communal sun. The pipes cool
when they're gone, swab clean
in the pause between
shifts and men who breathe coal.

ABERFAN FIFTY YEARS ON

Logic sees a slag-heap tipped out
over a stream as the shouting
afterwards, pet names
reaching through the shame
of it, claiming back what

can't answer. The same warnings ask
over and again, keep asking,
returning empty
handed. The simple
facts exemplify, mask,

ring hollow, measured against black
over snapped angles. It retracts
with time, becomes green
canals and serene
moments gleaned from the cracks

in old news. New families build
over the years, join those who've held
on. The graveyard slides
down the hill riding
time with wide-eyed children.

MERMAID DROWNING WENDY

(after the picture by Paula Rego, 1992)

A hand on each collar-bone forces
Wendy down, leaves her gagging. Words
burst in her mind, lose
touch. The world closes
as her ghosts resurface

in twists of salt. No clear image
but an ageless power, glimmers
of scale, the same reek
seaweed acquires stretched
over rocks in timeless

sun. Privileged beginnings flash
across in a thrill of splashes
and foam. London parks.
become miracles
of tree-dark and precious

green. Avenues breathe, forgetting
back-alleys, before they settle
into tricks of shade
and shine, the parade
of a glad-eyed sweetness,

not of memories, but the myths
between them. A broken rhythm
dances in the froth
of waves. The land floats
lights. A boat takes its berth

against rings and buoys, the pulsing
scream of gulls. From the shore, they roll
and they're gone. A tail
cracks like a loose sail,
slides down, swallowed, folded

away. Wendy's dress flourishes
and mushrooms on her unhurried
glide. Tomorrow's sand
or shingle demands
to be tangled with curls.

THE BLUE FAIRY WHISPERS TO PINOCCHIO
(after the picture by Paula Rego, 1996)

Dusting energy on the polished forehead
adds a little lustre, persuades the muscles
loose enough to conjure a frown. The simple
flick of a wand-tip

also works on hair, transforming the lifeless
bristles sewn or glued into place, inspiring
glances close to glittering ads, the posters
grinning the morning

back to sleep from every angle. Gawky
limbs remember life, or imagine, twitching
out of cramps and comas. The fingers wriggle
free from their decades

creaking into blossom. The mouth relaxes,
grins, begins to taste, as a word untangles
from the tongue. His first as a boy, a clumsy
syllable hardly

worth the effort, approaches understanding,
stumbles on connections. Inert beads dazzle
light, explore the glimmer of shape and surface,
coax him to tremble

fingers, risk a touch. She could stop him halfway
but she won't, or can't, having felt the warming
breath against her face. It's her dress, her whispered
welcome that matters

now he's here to nurture and love. Her echo
fills his mind with promises, thrives in broken
darkness, guides and coaxes. His answers come back
wearing the static

scars of ancient vinyl. The voice is someone
else's clothes, the smoker's staccato crackle
played for empty barstools, but his, or seems it,
now that the cadence

starts to fit. She smiles with a mother's clumsy
pride and takes his delicate hands, calling them
hers and hers alone. When he smiles an answer
something stays frozen.

ABORTION TRIPTYCH, LEFT-HAND PANEL

(after the picture by Paula Rego, 1998)

A plastic chair and a plastic bucket
dominate a room, a bed with hospital
wheels. Green walls exacerbate the sense
of a peace having settled, a tension
having snapped. A young woman with crossed
ankles lies doubled, keeps her knees tucked

beneath her. The rest amounts to hollowing
out, attempting to persuade herself
the knife inside might be from a room
in another life. Any assuming
further just adds salt to the deep stealth
of the drip dripping. Increasing cold

from somewhere, not a draught, but the shiver
of a name chosen and then let go
the way of buried streams. Not a memory
quite, an impression of closeness shimmers
through tiles and naked function. The glow
touches and slides from surfaces, giving

with curves, following like the girl's ripped
and soiled gingham. Movement from the corridor
outside suggests much the same as happened
here. Agreements mutter in the background,
each contracted to the sweating wards
where realities begin to slip.

A BIRTHDAY POEM FOR PAULA REGO

The tune is either one of her own
or a snippet from the radio
in her father's study, as she works
her pastels into life, hums through dark
and light. Animals fidget and pad
the border between worlds as the frown

of concentration lifts, then threatens
a smile. The little girl is herself
and a host of others from stories
handed down, whispers and the corners
of thought. Her animals are all there
for her birthday party, completing

the cast for the latest drama. Hens
and geese scrabble for food. Dogs also
steal in from the yard and neighbouring
farms. A chaos of limbs fights for space
and the gentle haven of shallows
where there was always dazzle to spend

on the waves and split the gloom. The girl
knows the shapes of her characters' dreams
depend on her and on themselves. Each
imago howls or grins the weakness
and strength of those the little girl sees
around her. Or not. She stops. It's hers,

she reminds herself, between a laugh
and that smile, and the world's, only once
she says it is. Her hands are a storm
of colours, as vivid and as warm
as fresh hearts. You can't help being fond
having felt the rip of giving birth.

FAMILY GROUP AT THE NEXT TABLE

We've a corner of the pub to ourselves
until a young woman
turns up, careful, helping
what we assume

correctly to be her grandmother,
guiding her to the table
beside us. Seemingly as planned
the men delay

their arrival a couple of minutes
before settling
into the same pattern. The glint
moistens and sweetens

into the tears you have to wipe
away hearing them ask
the granddad what he'd like
to drink, asking

again a little louder,
no doubt already
aware. His voice has the studied
quality, the red

of former industrial buildings
daubed with sunset,
taking his time. You feel it
more once

he forces the words out,
Half a B,
his usual. We could talk about
anything, but won't compete

with what we can hear. He's missed
the younger man,
the grandad has, missed him
and everything he means,

based on what the women
say. No need
to look, I can feel what's coming
as your knuckles knead

away at your eyes again,
two years
give or take, since the pain
of a loss that's still here.

THE DANCE OF HUNTER AND PREY

(for the R.S. Thomas and M.E. Eldridge Festival)

A thing of hunger and hinges
makes God the mechanic. Angles
and need spring from calm to life,
home on a moment's weakness, rip
and tear. Watched from a separate
realm, escaping the bright gift

of a glance, the hunter scans
the watcher in return. He stands
with the landscape unsteady
in binoculars, observing
and observed, weighing the curve
of flight. Nerves tune in to need

as the hunter obeys that drive
wired inside. Death is a given
as belief wrestles itself
into the calm of acceptance,
splitting the difference that keeps
life one step behind. A wealth

of permutations sound off, ring
through the trees. Each jingled
response brings the watcher back
to the role of the divine hand, bones
and structures inspired by breath blown
through them. One and the same lack,

once either hunter or prey drape
undone. Between each synaptic
pause, the papery light tweaks
the general run of stone walls,
fields where the crows gather. The cool
of the folded quiet speaks.

R.S. THOMAS AT ABERDARON

(for the R.S. Thomas and M.E. Eldridge Festival)

To see his shadow sketch the rocks
in his own image, unlocks and invokes
wonderment, a fleeting sense
in the face of time extending

all the way back to his first whiff
of God. The sea gathers and heaves
between cliffs and bays,
hoisting gulls and spray

above themselves. From here, the haul
of tankers and fishing boats rolls
out of importance. This could be,
and is, his edge, his hold on

a myth of stasis, the comfort blanket
of knowing no-one lasts. The hankering
for what never was
has its place among the ghost

voices, detached cries. His birth
and upbringing clash beneath the surface
of dead mines. Not here
but in the south, where the nervous

heaps and wheels waste into postcards
and flowers. God, if he knew them, has lost
track, holed up with the man
who wears his collar and stands

against the change, hides when he hears
parishioners, speaks Welsh at those tourists
he can't avoid. A sea
wind snatches freely

at his clothes and his hair. His shadow
dances to the same tune, straddles
the distance between his worlds,
oblivious to the raw cold.

STUBBING WHARF AT HEBDEN BRIDGE

That it should have been on the list of places
flooded barely raises an eyebrow. Valleys
cut as deep and hard as this steady tumble
down from the moorland

tend to gather more than their share of turmoil
somehow. Darkness dominates even airy
rhododendron days. It's as if the present
never escapes mines

decades out of sorts, or the mills converted
here and there from ghosts into garden-centre
tearooms. Heptonstall, or the ruffled graveyard
perching above it,

has its thumb-print here, and there's no concerted
urge to wipe it off, if the local bookshops
serve as any guide. You can feel the dead names
digging themselves in,

clinging on, refusing to let their words go
unremembered. Pushing between the pub doors,
both before and after the waters curdle
up from the canal,

breeds the same impression. Aware of corner
tables, benches, snugs as potential anchors
dropped by longer shadows than those of normal
structures, you can't help

looking back as well as across. You can't help
straining, just in case there's a hint of Boston
laughing, sobbing, arguing under thicker,
earthier accents

grouped around the bar. If it's getting gloomy
out especially, or the canal puckers
hints of rain. It passes as soon as not though
once we admit it.

MICHAEL 'WHISPERING DEATH' HOLDING

The bruise of a voice I've said before would suit
the sat-nav, if there's nowhere needs getting to
any time soon, registers the blemishing
of rain on the dregs of the day's sun. The pause
heralding recollection knows its impact
swells as long as the co-voice doesn't break in,
shatter its moment. *You know, there's a saying*
in the Caribbean, when there's rain and sun
the Devil and his wife are having a fight,
then laughing like every wooden cliché
that's ever heard a palm tree testing its weight
against so much time, or the music a boat
makes waiting on a bite. Veteran calm
amounts to that authority life exudes
looking back at an open pram.
   Evidence
of hazed achievement lopes towards the billboards
yards beyond the boundary rope. It begins
turning and limbering through initial strides,
elbows pigeon or seagull-style on the jog,
oozing into a more active gear, a wave
gathering momentum in, approaching white
daubed across, drawing the sling on the leather
seam. Past the bat in a flurry, skirmishing
with the pools of late shadows. And the long walk
back to the mark measured in the dirt with boots
born out of obligation. The same easing
from stillness again with the same flourish left
on the Jamaican air by the bat's split reed,
prelude to the dance of a smashed wicket.

Smiling
behind the mic, then letting the quiet chew
his latest pearl, when he resumes the flicker
of the rain is all gone. The closing session
will hardly change another thing. The umpires
will pick the bails from stumps, barter a mutter
with the bowlers, take the play home to the dark
collecting more precisely and more surely
at the fringes now. Summation will find him
expanded out of that ancient tone to life
on the studio floor. He'll answer when asked
but stay as far off, as unhurried as stands
once they're finally emptied out. The talking
pours him into a smile remembered by stamps
and the *chabby shubby* near Sabina Park.

GYMNASTICS — RIO 2016

Your feet are bouncing
in your flip-flops as you sit
watching the highlights
from Brazil. The sprung floor gives
and responds to the gymnasts

at each rotation,
propels them past what should be
possible. You step
across the time, feel the cold
and lifeless mats after school

as the music starts
again. Flexing, expressing
every move, feet
like a dancer's, you command
your universe. Perfect marks

as you finish, arch,
accept applause from the crowd
in your mind. The scores
filter down from the judges
for a British bronze. We're back

as we were, your feet
still dancing, the bony faces
of boys young enough
to be ours trying to get
to grips with what just happened.

ODE TO YOU AND NOT HOWARD WEBB

In the careful biro of one anxious
not to ruin the catharsis of your *Wank
Referee List*, I write
Howard Webb. With slight

adjustments for time and refereeing careers
not quite matching, he shares
notoriety with others
in need of a special offer

at a good optician. Not for the shirt
a size too tight, or the startling
resemblance to the lead singer
from *Right Said Fred*,

nor forgetting to count to two, or three,
or whatever it was meant to be,
in 2010. But, for pretending
to be nice, almost friendly,

as a panel guest on *BT Sport*,
saying *Yes, that really ought to have been
a Liverpool pen*. Like
he'd have done that at Anfield

in his day. Not that it matters,
of course. It's about us, not him,
and how neatly we fit,
and put all outstanding injustices right.

SNOOKER COMMENTARY

How much are they paying him
to tell me the winner gets
160 grand,
the loser, 60? This wannabe
Ted Lowe with wallpaper
charm, putting the dampeners
on the Rocket, chalky voice,
forcing me to watch
on mute. And yes, it could be
Terry Griffiths on one
of his *Eeyore* days, but even
then there's the wistful look back
over the shoulder at the valleys,
as seen through the hiraeth
of a postman's morning breath,
something to write home about,
rather than making me want
to rip off my one good ear.

WEAK LIGHT — DURHAM

Morning offers the weak light
of autumn, even before you find me
rising from a dream. The lines
of something half-remembered

hover a while, then vanish. Words
find their other halves loaded,
fired back with good
intent. The preparation

completes itself by now, checks
aside. Left to our own devices
we know the ritual as the difference
between worlds, the portal

beyond which the road unravels
into blue miles. A note rings
in my mind, a tingling
forever, a Baker or a Davis

for no reason outside itself
and heading towards the next unknown.

A SUNDAY MORNING IN COOKHAM

It's as his winter-haired self
he returns, the click of wheels,
pushing his pram and its wealth

of props and canvas. Or held
in the local mind, stopping
at the fringe of a ripe field

shifting from dark to light. Crops
shiver apart revealing
a glimpse of earth opening

into life, the village peeled
from work-a-day and dressing
in its Sunday best. The real

meaning of all those treasured
photographs, nailed to the walls
of the cottages he passed

on his way, comes back. Solid
suits and fob-watches hold still
until they're told to move. Folds

give structure to dresses, styles
from before the First War. Hands
are somewhere between idle

and occupied. The landscape
slips into gardens and bursts
sunflowers. The great stand-off

between then and the corner
of now he and the surface
share creaks a little. Morning

survives. The first unearthing
from their stones stretch and find words
take time to recover. Nerves

twitch and tremble as they're stirred
by the old man's art. Bones fill
and remember who they were

before they were locked in smiles.

F.D.R. WALKS

For all his pumping iron, his sweating
like a fat summer, his kilos of props
and leg supports, his toppling over
and having to be righted by waiting
hands, the main highway remains another
world. From his avenue of dappled light
birds scatter or catch in the branches, voice
their unconcern. Meditations shoot back
collections stuffed in their cases, medals
loitering after wars, constellations
of stamps. When it's too much, his chair accepts
his weight, tilts and corrects adventuring
roots. What traffic there is crosses behind
his return on a perpendicular
gradually lost to the leaves and the years
of planting. Tomorrow, providing war
allows, he'll start again, measure himself
against the same avenue, the same steps
unachieved. He'll brace, lean out, drag a leg,
drag a second, repeat, until he's done
trying. Until they carry him and lay him
where the *Springwood Rose Garden* takes its time
from the constant example of the sun.

MORECAMBE AND WISE SHOW

(Lowry Theatre, Salford)

Tonight revisits
Christmases past, raises ghosts
to crack those old jokes
about Des O'Connor, drop

invisible eggs
into brown paper bags, slap
and tickle past-lives
out of fireside slumber. Drive

the thought of traffic
out of our minds, enter lit
dark, the half-hush, take
our places and give ourselves

over to the balm
of nostalgia. We owe
ourselves these pleasures,
after so much else, the sweets

also, tucked away
in your pocket. As the lights
slip behind the time
and our hands fumble their way

back to each other,
for tonight, at least, we can
and will believe, see
Eric and Ernie, risen

like sun on a dawn
frost, dovetailing as neatly
as they always did,
surfing ripples and echoes.

GARDENING BLIND

Feeling first for the soil, then life
a few palms further in, belief
grows. The dark anchors
itself between ranks
of stem hanging leaf

on a delicate breath. Dampness
fumbles into a soft clamour,
or a snap of twig,
between regular
and more flexible claims

on late summer. Her finger-tips
test for ripeness, gently unclip
from the next bud down,
knowing, once she's done,
they'll rebound and ripple

back towards her. Her basket
never leaves her side, cuts the mask
a fresh hole. She piles
harvest on willow
bark until the basket

threatens to brim over, pats down
after every fifth handful,
smiling as she sniffs
what the clippings leave
her to gather and drain.

WINTER RAINBOW

Increasing with the morning's stretch
of uncommon blue, the moment
may as well have been waiting
for us to register, then communicate,
hardly needing to, clumsy
by comparison. Multiply perfection

by the fact we've had so few
good, even moderate
days this winter,
and we're only beginning to hint
at what it means, straddling
the view from your dad's room

in particular. You know the Bible
has it down as a promise,
don't you? between man and God,
and the weather, I suppose. We can add
between a man and his daughter, assume it
more beauty and ride it

further still. A room
like your dad's knows years more
of love and what the sun makes
of water than the pictures you take
to show me it was there. It wears
its meaning like a summer

beside him, your arm curved
around his smile, his knowing
by heart exactly when the storm
comes. Nothing abnormal
written out, but allowing
those glimpses you both deserve.

CC FOOTAGE OF KW

(Hillsborough 15 *April 1989)*

The shape of a man frozen
rushing towards the boy
stops their afternoon
at half past three
by an on-screen clock. The seconds
roll to his kneeling close
beside him on the Yorkshire turf,

fingers pressed to the tremor
in his neck. He'll be joined
by another who'll work on his crushed
chest while he tries to breathe him
back. An ambulance will blur
past, unstopping, with the driver
also caught in a loop

to be picked apart. The boy
will be given up on, carried
on a hording to a gym-cum-morgue
and tried again. *Mum*
will pop in his mouth. A woman
PC will hear him
at just gone four

and learn to call it hope
instead, to say she heard
because she wanted to
and her head was gone. The man
who ran to help will be wound on
and taken back, told
his fingers didn't touch a life,

the boy wasn't convulsing
when he found him, he hadn't
ticked beneath his skin
as if he might be more,
the ambulance was not the one
he heard and saw and tried
to flag down. Minutes

will be trimmed to fit a line
at which the boy was dead
before he spoke and blinked,
him and those others
the clock will go back on
to quarter past the truth
of their having had chances.

PRIMARK SOCKS

A note tucked neatly
between two socks unravels
into the same plea
repeated inside concrete
walls. If genuine, a male,

thirty-nine, loyal
to Chairman Xi Jinping, lives
under guard, or fills
a quiet hole. Officials
visit on their rounds, return

him to his childhood
with tedious eyes. A door
closes on the thought
of other slips of paper
ripped and thrown away, taken

for labels, hidden
to be found. Finer details
of a family
confined, a father killed off,
compete with a price-tag stamped

on a stitch, cotton
and nylon mix. The writer
checking, re-checking
across his shoulder, stuffs words
into a trusted hand, knows

somehow they'll wind up
at shelves and aisles. They reach back
to their fountain-head
of stolen ink, demand, beg
to be noticed, repeated.

THE BOATS

The ribbons make flags
on close inspection, not shirts
for the skeleton
inhabitants. The daubed words
on the creaking hulls confirm

the People's Army,
Korea. No fishing gear
to speak of, just drifts
obliging the flotilla
towards port and the lit coast

of Japan, gentle
sand, or a rocky spike. Time
lost sight of them shores
ago. They stare up and out
over relative calm, gape

the dark of nights lost
inside themselves. Weather carves
their gazing deeper
until they're disentangled
where they're taken in, guessed at.

SCOTLAND AS WE LEFT IT

Whenever we're wanting
for peace, the same place returns
more than we left there
when last we went that way. Trees
drift scatterings and litter

the roads. Mists raise ghosts
from an absent thought. Squirrels
work the branches thin
scratching for food. Deer are there
and gone. Sweeter cleaner air

compensates and saves
its best for us. When we wait
outside and you tilt
the stars for me to see them
from our own angle, a cooler

breath sweeps in. We lose
and find ourselves in the change
before night calls us
in. Whatever we left waits
ajar, bathes in the half-light.

BLACK GROUSE

Survivors, apparently safe
and impervious to the lash of weather
congregate, peck, stiffen,
raise their heads,
settle again. Their difference
draws us to their huddle

and their absolute black. Our pictures
compete with the mist, select
what detail they can. Next time
we look, they're heather
and brown stubble, protected
from themselves, leaving us

clutching at another first,
for us, at least. They'll resurface
once we're gone, more careful
perhaps, but driven
by the need to scratch and unearth
smatterings of life.

WITH THE FISHERWOMAN OF NAIRN

She could be one of crowds
similarly laden
with the latest catch, proud
against the steady
line of the pier, the muddle
of tides. A breed
apart, with the spark and the blood
cooled, she heads

a list of the pictures we take
home, joins
black grouse, relaxes
between sun-drenched
mountains. Her creel smacks
of success gone
west, as well as the lacklustre
sob of wandering

gulls. We leave her mute
statement, in favour
of time together with the remote
horizon, the gathered
mass of the next floating
headland. Tethered
moorings and idle boats
also breathe

their stillness for us, frame
our returning view,
the same fisherwoman
and her stenchless, unmoving

baskets. Today can be somewhere
for us to choose
above the world, a promise
to the clear blue.

This time, it would be so different. There would be no curling under and refusing to eat, no inevitable conclusion, and no need for the guilt, after 'rescuing' from the wild, one of the young bundles of life gathered somewhere near their nests. What was it about them, that just refused to live, however much care she gave them? Her dad always said something about sheep doing the same thing, making up their minds to die. She tried partridges, blackbirds, you name it, always with the same result, the stiff cold copy of a bird, she had to bury in the garden, in so little dirt. All apart from one injured starling. That one did survive, even coming back to her finger for weeks afterwards, its body and wings dazzling like winter stars.

If the starling could do it, maybe that magpie could as well. Not only was the magpie old enough and strong enough to last, it was used to people. That much was obvious, from the time that the boy, a few doors down, had spent training the bird, first of all to come into his garden, then come inside his house, and, at last, to take food from his hands.

The little girl waited. There would be a day when the magpie sat on her garden fence again, before returning to the house a few doors down. It had happened at least twice, after all, and without anything to tempt the bird there. How much easier would it be if she…?

She placed bread and milk in the garden, went back indoors, until she had to go to school. Nothing, for the first days, the first week. But she replaced the milk and bread each morning, and watched as long as she could. Then summer, the holidays, and all that beautiful stretched time. Not just bread and milk, but scraps of meat by then too, just like it said in the nature book in her father's bookcase. A magpie was a crow, a colourful one, and she always saw crows around any animals killed on the roads.

And then it happened. A dull morning spat the magpie onto the fence. After a few seconds cocking its head on one side, then the other, the bird, *her* bird, hopped onto the patio stones, gobbled the bread and meat, dabbed at the milk. With the offerings a few yards closer, the following morning, the bird returned, dropping straight down, any sign of nerves gone.

How, then, to coax him, (she decided it had to be him), into the house, either by the window, or the back door? How to do it without her mother and her father noticing, for the time being, at least? Perhaps, another week of gifts, bringing the magpie closer and closer to the backdoor, the kitchen. And then more gifts left out on the kitchen floor, or the windowsill. The week passed without a hitch, despite that one morning when the girl had to go to the dentist instead, and there was no milk or bread. Day seven, and she chose the windowsill, leaving the window open, and placed a little extra milk on the kitchen table, along with the glitter of a milk bottle top.

Sitting perfectly still, at the far end of the kitchen, the girl knew that, after today, nothing could ever be the same. She would always feel the acid bite in her chest, hear her own blood-rush, every time the magpie crossed her mind, or appeared as another of its kind, among the tree-jostle of parks and roadsides. The familiar stoop, and cocked beak, tweezered through the windowsill's offerings, before settling at the table, jabbing at the milk bottle top, and flying clean through the open window, with its prize.

Two weeks on, and he was hers, part of her sleeping and waking, her rhythm, coming to hand, to take his fill, never more than a glance away from her, following from room to room, waiting outside on the fence for the window to open. This despite her mother's initial horror at the thought, and her father's reminder that perhaps a bird like that would be happier in the wild. Both softened, if not entirely believing the girl's answers that the bird had lost its mother, and had nowhere else to go. One night, that's all, her mother made her promise, when the girl asked her if the magpie could stay.

Happy, for the most part, to perch on the armchair beside the girl, but taking the odd scuttled flight around the room, the bird watched, chose its moment, launched itself towards the girl's mother. Or, more accurately, the girl's mother's head. Shrieking, arms flapping, the girl's mother tried to scare it off.

The girl's earthy chuckle could no more help itself, than clouds or sunlight can help being what they are.

'It thinks your hair is a nest,' the girl managed to tell her mother, between giggles. 'It wants to be your friend.'

'I don't care. Get it off me. Get it out.'

But the more her mother panicked, the more the magpie's claws got tangled, knotted up in the mass of curls. The screams got louder, coming from the bird now, as well. Feathers, shining like wet tar, scattered in spirals. The girl's father tried to help, reaching out towards the bird. The bird pecked at his hand, drawing blood, and causing him to back away, wrapping his fingers in his shirt.

Only when the girl approached did the magpie settle again, fixing its black gaze on her, and allowing her clever fingers to unravel him from the mesh of hair.

Having been recaptured, escorted to the kitchen, and ordered out, the magpie leapt from the girl's hand, back into flight and its other world. The girl felt the joy and sorrow of it rolling down her cheek, as a single hot tear. If her mother hadn't made such a fuss, if she hadn't scared the bird, he would still have been there.

For the best, apparently, or at least according to the girl's parents. Not that it stopped the girl watching from the kitchen every morning, tracing flight paths between perching posts. Sometimes, when she was outside, the girl could swear that the magpie was there, observing, studying, half-expecting more food. She guarded her secret, cherished both the sensation and the thought. She would never forgive her mother, never. For weeks she wouldn't talk to her mother, wouldn't even look at her, going back inside the house whenever her mother came out to tend and pluck the garden.

The silence grew, feeding off itself. The house succumbed to an awkward calm. The girl, her mother, and her father, drifted between their own routines. The girl went for long walks most days, sometimes coming back only when it was dark. Her mother carried on, pruned, and clipped, tried to heal the division. Her father tried to tell his daughter, again, there would be other pets, other lives to which she could make a difference.

Back home early, one afternoon, from her walk in the woods, and for no reason that she could really explain, the girl poured herself a glass of milk, chose a quiet corner and a book buzzing with nature. The magpie page fell open, caught in the sunlight.

This time, when they reached her, the screams were different, more desperate. The girl ran out into the garden, saw her mother with her hands raised to her face, blood soaking her skin.

The magpie rested on its favourite fence-post, juggling with an eye and an optic nerve, swallowed the parcel whole.

ACKNOWLEDGEMENTS II

This book would not have been possible without the support, friendship and love of a number of people, to all of whom I could not be more grateful, including Anthony Rudolf, Michael Schmidt, Jon Glover, Richard Berengarten, W.D. Jackson, Noreen Kershaw, Sam Holland, Sally Carman, Lucy Thatcher, Francis Tucker, Erin Shanagher, Bernard Wrigley, Barbara Dickson, Sue Johnston, Ricky Tomlinson, Tim Pollard, Roger Appleton, LA Productions, Colin McKeown, Donna Molloy, Dame Paula Rego, Keith Hutson, Kath Osgerby, Elspeth Billie Penfold, Eileen Gunn, Clive Twist, David Riding, Vicki Holland, Dani and the Banegas family, Sybil Lowery, Terri-Louise and David Maher, Jake and Thomas Winstanley, Margaret Earnshaw, and my wife, Jayne, so often my rock and my inspiration. Thank you all so much. Thank you also to the wonderful people at Unlimited/Shape Arts, Regain Sports Charity, the Regional Spinal injuries Unit at Southport, Liverpool Football Club, and Northern House and Carcanet Press.

I must also thank the Royal Literary Fund, the Society of Authors and the Author's Foundation for their generous and life-changing support.